KNOWLEDGE ENCYCLOPEDIA
DINOSAUR!

DK

LONDON, NEW YORK, MELBOURNE, MUNICH, AND DELHI

DK UK:

Senior Art Editor Stefan Podhorodecki

Senior Editors Francesca Baines, Jenny Sich

Project Editor Steven Carton

Art Editor Paul Drislane

Managing Art Editor Michael Duffy

Managing Editor Linda Esposito

Publisher Andrew Macintyre

Jacket Design Development Manager Sophia MTT

Jacket Designer Laura Brim

Jacket Editor Maud Whatley

Producer (Pre-Production) Luca Frassinetti

Producer Gemma Sharpe

DK Picture Library Romaine Werblow

Art Director Phil Ormerod

Associate Publishing Director Liz Wheeler

Publishing Director Jonathan Metcalf

DK India:

Senior Art Editor Anis Sayyed

Editorial team Priyanka Kharbanda, Deeksha Saikia, Rupa Rao

Project Art Editor Mahipal Singh

Art Editors Vikas Chauhan, Vidit Vashisht

Jacket Designer Suhita Dharamjit

DTP Designer Vishal Bhatia

Picture Researcher Surya Sarangi

Managing Editor Kingshuk Ghoshal

Managing Art Editor Govind Mittal

Managing Jacket Editor Saloni Singh

Pre-Production Manager Balwant Singh

Production Manager Pankaj Sharma

First published in Great Britain in 2014 by
Dorling Kindersley Limited,
80 Strand, London WC2R 0RL

A Penguin Random House Company

A CIP catalogue record for this
book is available from the British Library.

ISBN: 978-1-4093-5467-3

Printed and bound in China

Discover more at
www.dk.com